D1090972

GREEN BERETS

BY NICK GORDON

BELLWETHER MEDIA · MINNEAPOLIS, MN

EPIC BOOKS are no ordinary books. They burst with intense action, high-speed heroics, and shadows of the unknown. Are you ready for an Epic adventure?

This edition first published in 2013 by Bellwether Media, Inc.

No part of this publication may be reproduced in whole or in part without written permission of the publisher. For information regarding permission, write to Bellwether Media, Inc., Attention: Permissions Department, 5357 Penn Avenue South, Minneapolis, MN 55419.

Library of Congress Cataloging-in-Publication Data

Gordon, Nick.
  Army Green Berets / by Nick Gordon.
     p. cm. – (Epic books: U.S. Military)
  Includes bibliographical references and index.
  Summary: "Engaging images accompany information about Army Green Berets. The combination of high-interest subject matter and light text is intended for students in grades 2 through 7"–Provided by publisher.
  Audience: Grades 2-7.
  ISBN 978-1-60014-823-1 (hbk. : alk. paper)
  1. United States. Army. Special Forces–Juvenile literature. I. Title.
  UA34.S64G67 2013
  356'.167–dc23   2012008557

Printed in the United States of America, North Mankato, MN.

A special thanks to milpictures.com for contributing images.

TABLE OF CONTENTS

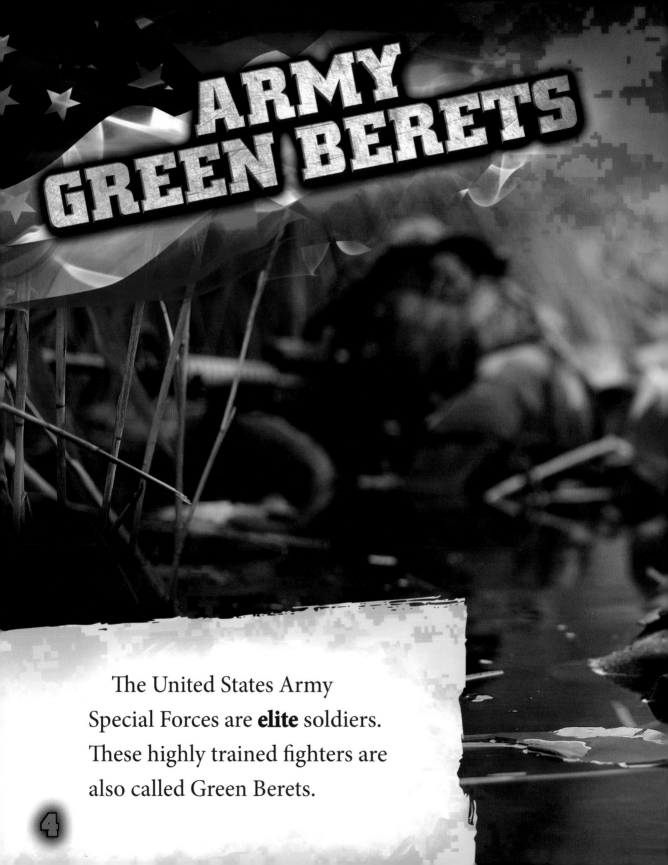

ARMY GREEN BERETS

The United States Army Special Forces are **elite** soldiers. These highly trained fighters are also called Green Berets.

GREEN BERET FACT

U.S. President John F. Kennedy called the Green Beret "a symbol of excellence, a badge of courage, a mark of distinction in the fight for freedom."

Green Berets carry out some of the Army's toughest **missions**. They fight **terrorists** and spy on enemies. They even train troops of U.S. **allies**.

ARMY GREEN BERETS

Founded: 1952

Headquarters: Fort Bragg, North Carolina

Motto: *De Oppresso Liber*
                     (To Liberate the Oppressed)

Size: About 5,500 active personnel

Major Engagements: Cold War, Vietnam War,
                     Operation Just Cause,
                     Gulf War, Somalia, Iraq War,
                     Afghanistan War

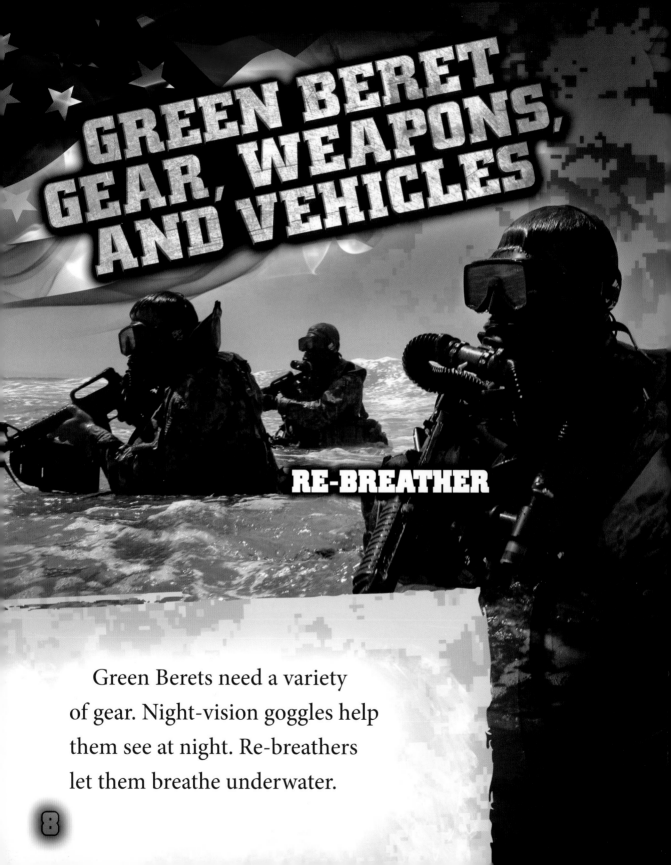

GREEN BERET GEAR, WEAPONS, AND VEHICLES

RE-BREATHER

Green Berets need a variety of gear. Night-vision goggles help them see at night. Re-breathers let them breathe underwater.

NIGHT-VISION GOGGLES

Green Berets use parachutes
to jump into enemy territory.
HALO helmets help them
breathe in thin air.

KEEP CLEAR OF CARGO DOORS

Green Berets carry several types of guns. The M4 **carbine** is the most common. The M9 pistol is often carried as a **sidearm**.

M4 CARBINE

M9 PISTOL

Green Berets must get around without being noticed. Helicopters carry them from place to place. Kayaks and inflatable boats help them move quietly over water.

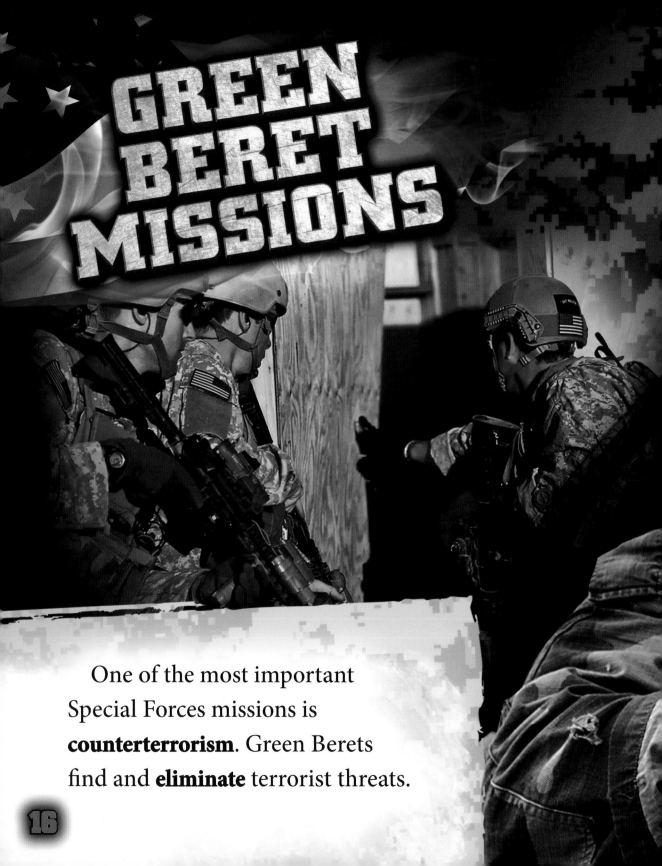

GREEN BERET MISSIONS

One of the most important Special Forces missions is **counterterrorism**. Green Berets find and **eliminate** terrorist threats.

Green Berets also take part in small, quick strikes on enemies. They sometimes rescue **hostages**.

GREEN BERET FACT

Every Green Beret must speak at least one foreign language.

19

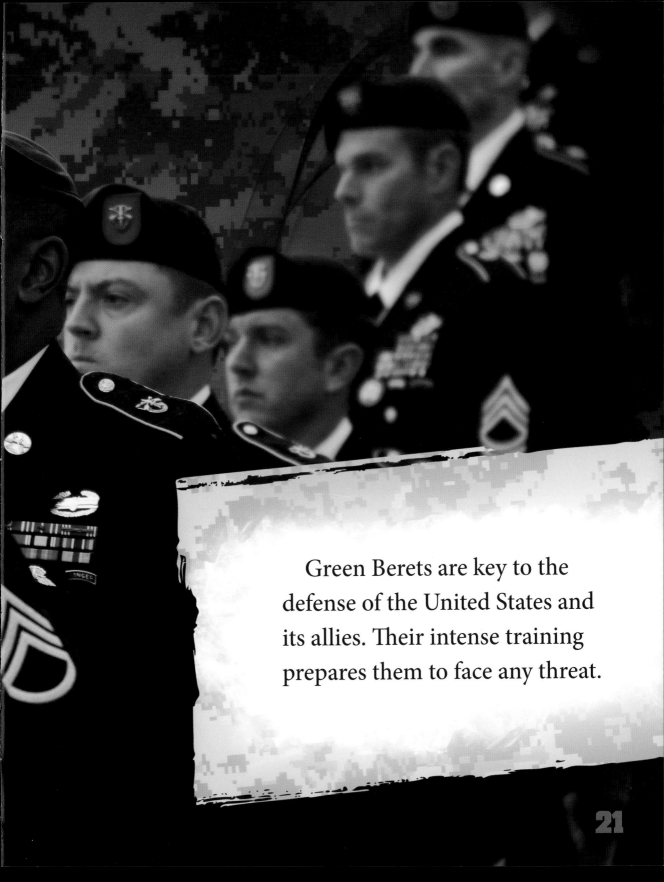

Green Berets are key to the defense of the United States and its allies. Their intense training prepares them to face any threat.

GLOSSARY

allies—friendly nations that have common goals or purposes; the United States has many allies around the world.

carbine—a lightweight rifle with a short barrel

counterterrorism—military action that combats terrorists

eliminate—to get rid of

elite—the most skilled

HALO helmets—special helmets that help Green Berets breathe at extreme heights

hostages—people who are captured and held in exchange for something

missions—military tasks

sidearm—a second weapon that is worn on one's side

terrorists—those who perform violent acts to create fear among people

TO LEARN MORE

At the Library

Besel, Jennifer M. *The Green Berets*. Mankato, Minn.: Capstone Press, 2011.

David, Jack. *Army Green Berets*. Minneapolis, Minn.: Bellwether Media, 2009.

Gordon, Nick. *U.S. Army*. Minneapolis, Minn.: Bellwether Media, 2013.

On the Web

Learning more about Army Green Berets is as easy as 1, 2, 3.

1. Go to www.factsurfer.com.

2. Enter "Army Green Berets" into the search box.

3. Click the "Surf" button and you will see a list of related Web sites.

With factsurfer.com, finding more information is just a click away.

INDEX